MY FIRST ENCYCLOPEDIA

An eye-catching series of information books designed to encourage young children to find out more about the world around them. Each one is carefully prepared by a subject specialist with the help of experienced writers and educational advisers.

KINGFISHER
Kingfisher Publications Plc
New Penderel House, 283-288 High Holborn, London WC1V 7HZ

First published in paperback by Kingfisher Publications Plc 1994
2 4 6 8 10 9 7 5 3 1

1BP/0500/SF/(FR)/135MA

ISBN 1 85697 264 X

Phototypeset by Waveney Typesetters, Norwich
Printed in China

People Long Ago

Kingfisher

Authors
Dominique Joly and Christopher Maynard

History consultant
Sally Purkis

Series consultant
Brian Williams

Editor
Odette Dénommée

Designer
Anne Boyer

Illustrators
Louis R. Galante
Marc Lagarde
Florence McKenzie
Barry Mitchell
François Pichon,
Etienne Souppart
Valérie Stetten

What is history?

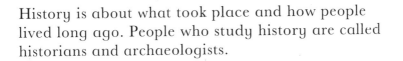

History is about what took place and how people lived long ago. People who study history are called historians and archaeologists.

Just like detectives, historians and archaeologists hunt for clues to the way people once lived. Bits of pottery, old monuments, weapons, written records – these all tell us about the past.

Then, very patiently, historians and archaeologists put the different bits and pieces together like a giant jigsaw puzzle. It is thanks to them that we know about the people and the events this book describes.

When an historical site is discovered, archaeologists uncover and record everything they find. Pieces of pottery and beautifully carved stones may have been lying buried for hundreds of years and must be dug out, slowly and gently. This picture shows archaeologists at work about 80 years ago.

CONTENTS

PREHISTORY
The first people 14
Wandering hunters 16
Village life 18
Amazing facts 20

THE ANCIENT WORLD
A merchant's notebook 22
Ancient Egypt 24
Pharaohs and gods 26
The Hebrews 28
Ancient India 30
Sailing by the stars 32
Ancient Greece 34
The first Olympic Games 36
The Roman Empire 38
Life in Rome 40
Christianity 42
Amazing facts 44

THE MIDDLE AGES

The invaders......................46
The Queen of Cities..........48
The Muslims.....................50
The Vikings 52
Castles of stone 54
Knights in armour 56
The Church 58
Bustling towns..................60
Amazing facts 62

AROUND THE WORLD

An imperial city 64
Warriors of Japan.............66
The Oba of Benin.............68
An Aztec city 70
Wealthy emperors.............72
Amazing facts 74

TIMES OF CHANGE

New ideas.........................76
European explorers...........78
Kings and queens 80
Moscow 82

Settlers in North America 84
War of Independence........ 86
Slavery 88
Australia........................... 90
The French Revolution 92
Amazing facts................... 94

 THE INDUSTRIAL
AGE

Coal and steam 96
The pioneers.................... 98
Steam trains 100
Cars and planes.............. 102
World War I................... 104
In the home 106
Revolution in Russia....... 108
World War II 110
Amazing facts................. 112

TODAY

The United Nations........ 114
Exploring Space 116
New inventions 118
Amazing facts................. 120

INDEX......................... 121

Prehistory

The first people

Human beings gradually grew taller

The first people appeared about two million years ago. They did not wear any clothes and lived in small groups. Some lived in caves, while others lived in simple shelters.

The first humans
learned how to
make fire and how
to make simple tools
out of stone. They
used these tools to
hunt animals and to
chop their food.

tools used by
the first people

Wandering hunters

Early people lived by
hunting. They had to
roam far and wide to
find the animals and
plants that were their
food. They made
shelters from branches
covered with animal skins.
These were easy to put up and
take down every time they moved on.

lamp

needle

spearhead

Once early people had learned to control
fire, life was easier.

Early people used bone needles to make clothes out of animal skins. A spear with a bone spearhead made a good hunting weapon.

Village life

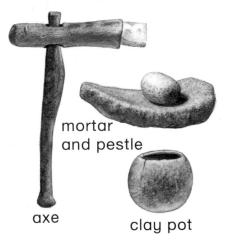

mortar
and pestle

axe

clay pot

A mortar and pestle
were used to grind
grain.

About 10,000 years
ago, people began
to keep flocks of
animals and to farm
the land. This gave
them a steady
supply of food and
wool. Now they
didn't have to roam
around all the time
to find their food.

Historians believe that giant circles of stones like this one were built for religious ceremonies. You can see the remains of these circles in places such as Stonehenge in England.

Instead, people began to settle in small villages. They wove wool to make clothes and made bowls out of clay, which they hardened in a fire. Their tools were made of wood, stone and bone. Later, they learned to make tools out of metal.

Amazing facts

No human being ever saw a dinosaur. Dinosaurs had vanished from the Earth many millions of years before the first people appeared.

Historians think the first people lived in Africa about two million years ago.

It takes about 100 taps to put a sharp edge on a stone chopper. This was the tool that the first people used for most jobs.

Some of the early people were skilled artists. They painted pictures of animals and hunting scenes on the walls of caves.

One of the first animals to live with humans was the dog. Wild dogs used to hang around settlements to get scraps of food, so some people think it was dogs who adopted humans, rather than humans who adopted dogs.

The Ancient

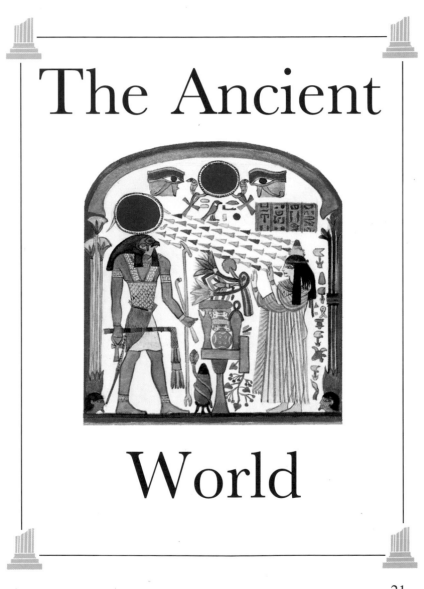

World

🏛 A merchant's notebook

In a land called Mesopotamia, in the Middle East, people settled and built the first cities in the world. Merchants came into the cities to trade their goods.

a merchant's clay tablet

The merchants kept records of what they traded by making marks on clay tablets. This is how writing first began, more than 5,000 years ago.

▶ Babylon was one of the great cities in Mesopotamia. The main city gate, called the Ishtar Gate, was decorated with pictures of dragons and bulls. Here, people met to talk and trade.

🏛 Ancient Egypt

Most of Egypt is desert, but one of the greatest rivers in the world, the Nile, runs through it. Once a year, the Nile flooded its banks, leaving behind a layer of rich soil. Here the Egyptians settled. Their empire lasted for almost 3,000 years.

Egyptian farmers dug irrigation channels to bring water from the river to their fields. There, they grew wheat and barley to make bread and beer, and flax to weave into cloth. From the marshes they gathered a reed called papyrus. They wove this to make many useful things, such as rafts, sandals and paper.

⬛ Pharaohs and gods

Some Egyptian gods

| Horus | Isis | Osiris | Re' | Anubis |

The Egyptians believed in many gods. They also believed that their ruler, the pharaoh, was a god. When he died, he was buried with piles of treasure in a huge pyramid or in a great tomb cut into a cliff.

This gold mask covered the preserved body, or mummy, of Pharaoh Tutankhamun. The piles of treasure buried with him were for him to enjoy in the next world.

pyramid

 The Hebrews

The Hebrews were a tribe of people from the
area between Egypt and Mesopotamia.
They were nomads who moved around with
their flocks of sheep and goats. After
hundreds of years of wandering, they settled
and formed the Kingdom of Israel.

The Hebrews worshipped only one god.
The laws of their god were written on tablets
of stone. These heavy tablets were kept in
a box called the Ark of the Covenant,
which the Hebrews took wherever
they went.

⛪ Ancient India

In Ancient India, not everyone had the same religion. One group, the Hindus, believed that the River Ganges was a holy river. They came to bathe in it to wash away their sins. They also came to worship their different gods in temples decorated with many statues. Hinduism is still the main religion in modern India.

Another religious group in India was the
Buddhists. Buddhism was founded by a
man called Siddhartha Gautama about
2,500 years ago. Siddhartha Gautama
was inspired with his ideas while he was
meditating under a fig tree.

🏛 Sailing by the stars

The Polynesians were some of the greatest
sailors of all time. More than 3,000 years
ago, they were already sailing across the
huge Pacific Ocean in their catamarans to
find new islands to settle. They steered
by reading the stars, and by watching
the waves, the currents and
changes in
the wind.

Some Polynesian
people tattooed
their faces.

Ancient Greece

In Greece, a land of mountains, good farmland was rare, but the sea was never far away. The Ancient Greeks became great sailors and traders. They travelled far and wide to trade their wine, oil, pottery and jewellery for wheat, wood, ivory ...almost anything.

About 2,500 years ago, Athens was
the richest Greek city of all.
Its famous temple, the
Parthenon, stood
high above the
city and its busy
market-place.

🏛 The first Olympic Games

Like the Egyptians, the Greeks had many gods. They held big festivals to honour them. The mightiest of all the gods was Zeus. Special games were held at Olympia every four years in his honour. Here, the best athletes competed in different events. These were the very first Olympic Games.

A crown of olive leaves was awarded to the best athlete.

Throwing the discus and the race in armour were two of the events in the ancient Olympics.

Athena

Zeus

Poseidon

Apollo

Some Greek gods

mask

Stories about the gods were told in plays that sometimes lasted from dawn to dusk. In Greek theatres, the actors wore masks. The audience sat on stone seats, looking down on the stage.

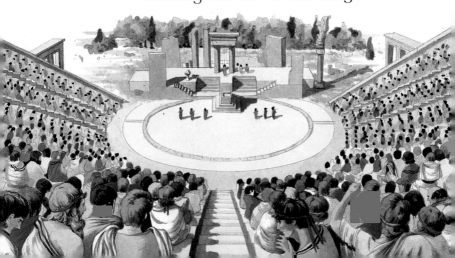

The Roman Empire

About 1,800 years ago,
the city of Rome was the
centre of the biggest empire anyone had
ever known. Roman soldiers had conquered
large parts of Europe and North Africa.

When the victorious army returned to Rome, it marched through the city to show off all the riches that it had captured.
Wherever they went, the Romans built long, stone-paved roads to link up the different parts of their empire.

🏛 Life in Rome

Rome was the greatest city of its time. At its biggest, it had almost one million inhabitants.

In the centre of the city was an open area called the Forum. The Forum was ringed by monuments: temples, statues, columns and splendid arches. Here, the citizens of Rome met to chat and to do business.

A slave helped a noble boy wash and dress.

At school he wrote his lessons on wax tablets.

Afterwards he could play with a hoop or knuckle-bones.

In the afternoon he might go to the public baths with his father.

🏛 Christianity

The Romans believed in many gods, but not all the people in their empire had the same religion. In Palestine, in the eastern part of the empire, a man called Jesus invited people to follow his beliefs.

Many people decided to follow Jesus' teachings and became Christians. Slowly, Christianity spread through the Roman Empire. At first it was banned. But in the end, most people in the Empire became Christians.

dove

Some early Christian symbols

lamb

fish

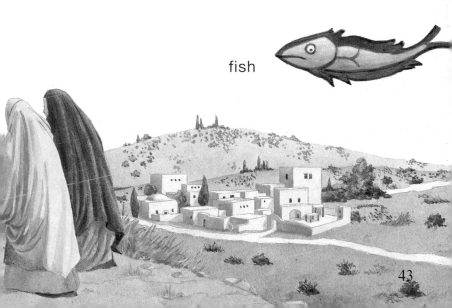

Amazing facts

About 70 years ago, the unopened tomb of the Egyptian pharaoh, Tutankhamun, was discovered. The treasures inside helped scientists and historians get a better idea of how the Ancient Egyptians lived.

People first started using coins about 2,700 years ago. Before that, traders exchanged goods. This was called bartering.

The Roman idea of entertainment was often very violent. At the Colosseum in Rome, as many as 100,000 people came to watch armed men called gladiators fight to the death. The floor of the Colosseum could also be flooded with water for mock sea battles and other spectacles.

The Middle

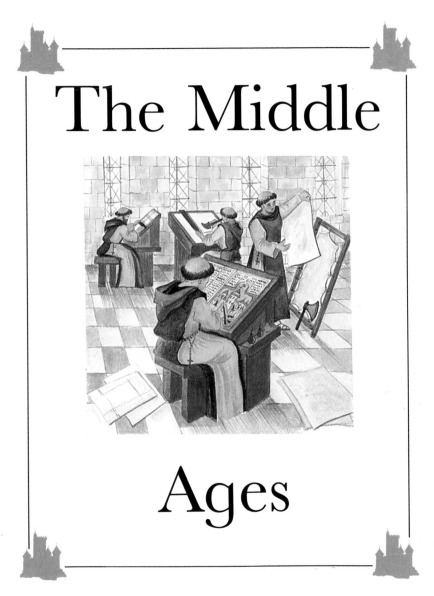

Ages

The invaders

Huns

At the height of its power, the Roman Empire stretched from Great Britain across Europe as far as the Middle East.

Angles

But many tribes of invaders kept attacking the Empire from the north and east. The Romans called these invaders barbarians.

Germans

After a time, the Roman Empire was defeated and split up into smaller kingdoms.

The barbarians mixed with the people of the old Empire.

Franks

The barbarians brought with them their own customs, laws and their skills in metalwork.

Visigoths

The Queen of Cities

Part of the Roman Empire survived in the east. Its capital was Constantinople (now called Istanbul). Here, merchants from the Far East, Europe and Africa met to trade and Constantinople soon became a very rich city. It was known as 'The Queen of Cities'.

Constantinople was protected by high stone walls. Inside, there were beautiful palaces and a great cathedral topped by a dome. The city's craftsmen were famous for their buildings and works of art.

Mosaics, like this one of the Empress Theodora, were made of tiny bits of coloured glass.

 # The Muslims

In Arabia, the prophet Muhammad, founded
the religion called Islam. Many Arabs
became followers of Islam, or Muslims.
When Muslim warriors invaded North Africa
and Spain, they took their religion with them.

Wherever they went, the Muslims built
mosques where they could pray to their god,
Allah. Their cities became centres of
learning, for they were great scientists and
were skilled in medicine and astronomy.

 The Vikings

In the cold lands of the north lived the Vikings. Most Vikings were farmers, but they were also fierce warriors who raided the coasts of Europe. They could row and sail great distances in their light, flat-bottomed ships, called longships.

Many Vikings set out in search of new farmland. They settled in France, Ireland, Scotland and the north of England. The Vikings were also skilled craftsmen and their ships were often decorated with beautiful carvings like this one.

prow of a Viking ship

Castles of stone

In Europe, in the Middle Ages, there were many wars, so landowners called lords lived with their families and soldiers in castles. The first castles were built of wood. Later, they were made of stone with a deep ditch, or moat, all the way around the outside.

The peasants who farmed the lord's land lived in villages nearby. But in times of danger, they came into the castle for protection.

In wartime, soldiers stood guard in towers spaced along the castle wall.

Knights in armour

A lord had many soldiers called knights to serve him if he went to war. In peacetime, the knights needed to keep in training. Sometimes they travelled to tournaments, where they could take part in mock battles and compete against each other in jousts.

A knight's training started early. At 6, he learned to ride and shoot. At 14, he became a squire and learned how to fight. At 18, he became a knight.

 The Church

In Europe, in the Middle Ages, the Christian Church was very rich and powerful. Unlike most people, monks and nuns could read and write. They copied out books by hand and decorated them with illustrations. Monks and nuns were the only teachers too, but few people went to school.

▶ Kings and Church leaders spent a lot of money building great cathedrals. Thousands of craftsmen came from far and wide to work on them.

59

# Bustling towns

Most European towns about this time were surrounded by high stone walls. But inside, nearly all the buildings were made of wood.

The narrow, muddy streets were crowded with loaded carts, and cows, sheep and pigs on their way to market. Shops and workshops opened straight onto the street. Shops that sold the same goods were grouped together in the same part of town.

Amazing facts

A knight's armour weighed about as much as a ten-year-old child. On top of that, he also had to carry a heavy sword and shield.

People did not eat off plates or use forks in the Middle Ages. Instead, they used their fingers to eat. The food was served on long slabs of bread.

Houses in the Middle Ages were dark and gloomy. Windows were tiny and were covered over with oiled paper. Glass windows were too expensive.

It took the wood of 8,000 oak trees to build even a small castle.

Around the

world

Outside Europe, other empires had
developed. Emperors ruled over a great
empire in China. In 1421, the emperor
moved his court to the city of Beijing.
He lived with his family and thousands of
servants in a walled palace as big as a town.

The palace was called the Forbidden City,
because no-one except the emperor's
household was allowed inside. In the streets
of Beijing, craftsmen wove silk cloth and
painted porcelain bowls. China was famous
for its silk and porcelain.

Warriors of Japan

In Japan, about **400** years ago, fierce warriors called samurai served their overlords by fighting in their wars. To protect them in battle, the samurai wore armour made of metal plates and leather.

Japan was not just a country of war. It had many beautiful ceremonies and traditions too. One of these was the tea ceremony. People wore special robes and followed strict rules for this ceremony.

 # The Oba of Benin

The Benin people were famous for their sculpture.

About 500 years ago, Benin was one of the most powerful kingdoms in Africa. Its people worshipped their king, the oba, as if he were a god. The oba owned all the land in the country and his word was law.

Every year, for three months, the oba travelled around with his chiefs, dressed in his rich royal robes. All kinds of ceremonies were held during this time.

# An Aztec city

In America, two great empires had
developed. The Incas lived in what is now
Peru, in South America. In what is now
Mexico, the Aztecs ruled over a great
kingdom from their capital, Tenochtitlán.

Girls prepare incense for a ceremony.

Tenochtitlán was built on islands in the middle of a marshy lake. Canals criss-crossed the city. In the centre stood great pyramid-shaped temples where priests performed ceremonies for the Aztec gods.

Priests were often teachers too. Here, a priest teaches children to play musical instruments.

 Wealthy emperors

About 450 years ago, horsemen from the
north invaded India and founded the Mogul
Empire. The Mogul emperors lived in
beautiful palaces topped with golden domes.
Their gardens were filled with fruit trees and
splashing fountains.

The greatest Mogul emperor was Akbar. Akbar invited many artists and musicians to his court to work for him. Akbar was a wise and just ruler. He was a Muslim, but he allowed the many Hindus in his empire to worship their gods as they wished.

Amazing facts

The Great Wall of China was built more than 2,000 years ago to protect China from invaders. It measures nearly 6,400 kilometres and is the longest wall ever built.

In Japan, everyone had to show respect to a samurai warrior, otherwise he could kill you on the spot!

The words avocado, chocolate and tomato all come from the Náhuatl language. This was the language spoken by the Aztecs more than 500 years ago.

The Mogul emperor, Shah Jahan, loved his wife so much that, when she died, he built a beautiful building in white marble over her grave. The building was the Taj Mahal.

Times of

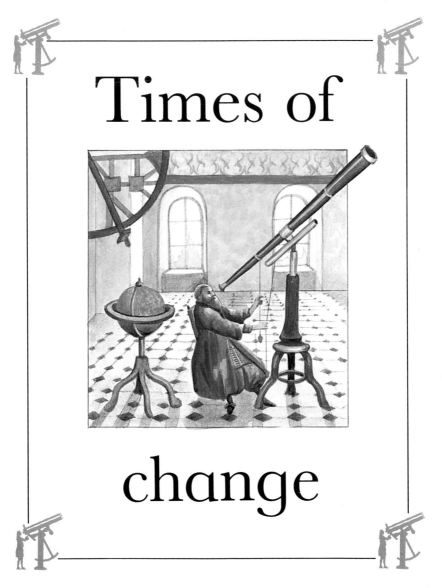

change

Around 1450, people in Europe started to take a great interest in learning. They studied the world they lived in and made important discoveries in science and astronomy. Artists also found new ways of showing what they saw around them.

76

The new ideas and knowledge spread
quickly, helped by the invention of printing.
People felt as if a new age had begun.
That is why this period is often called the
Renaissance – Renaissance is a French word
that means rebirth.

European explorers

The new ideas of the Renaissance also led to an interest in exploration.

caravel

Better sailing ships and new instruments for navigating meant that sailors were able to make longer voyages. Kings and queens encouraged explorers to go and discover new lands and riches. Europeans sailed to Africa, India, the West Indies and America for the first time.

European explorers used new kinds of sailing ships such as the caravel, the carrack and the nao for their long ocean voyages.

nao

carrack

Kings and queens

Elizabeth the First,
Queen of England

At this time, most of the countries of Europe were ruled by kings and queens. Kings and queens had almost complete power over their countries.

The kings and queens of Europe built elegant new palaces for themselves and their courts. Philip the Second of Spain built a great palace called the Escorial outside his capital, Madrid.

Philip the Second, King of Spain

Louis the Fourteenth, King of France

But perhaps the grandest palace of all was Versailles, home of the French king, Louis the Fourteenth.

 # MOSCOW

In Russia, the king was called the tsar. He lived in the capital, Moscow. The heart of Moscow, called the Kremlin, was surrounded by a wall. The most beautiful buildings, including the tsar's palace and several churches, were inside the Kremlin.

Outside the Kremlin walls, the ordinary people lived in houses built of logs. These wooden houses caught fire easily. Sometimes fire spread from house to house so quickly that half the city went up in flames.

Settlers in North America

More than 350 years ago, a group of people from England landed in North America to settle there. They were not the first people to live in North America. Tribes of Native Americans had been living there for thousands of years.

The settlers farmed the land and traded with the Native Americans for furs. Over the years their farms grew. Ships filled with wood, tobacco and sugar from their farms sailed across to Europe.

Although the settlers lived so far away, they were still ruled by the King of England and had to pay him taxes.

War of Independence

As time went by, the settlers in North America no longer wanted to pay taxes to the King of England.

To protest against a tax on tea, settlers (wearing disguises) raided three English ships in Boston Harbour and threw their cargo of tea overboard.

This was a signal for other settlers to join a revolt. After six years of fighting, the English were defeated and the settlers became independent. A new country was born; it was called the United States of America. People across the new country celebrated their victory by parading behind their new flag.

 Slavery

The European settlers in America needed many workers to farm their crops of cotton, tobacco, sugar cane and rice. This led to a huge trade in slaves from Africa.

People were captured on the west coast of Africa, then chained up in ships and taken to America. There they were sold as slaves. Many of them died on the way.

Over the years, about 15 million Africans were shipped to North and South America before slavery was finally banned and all the slaves set free.

In the 1700s, European explorers began to map the Pacific Ocean. Scientists went with them to study the animals and plants of lands such as Australia.

Aborigine painting

Tribes of Aborigines had already been living in Australia for thousands of years. They hunted animals for food and were skilled painters. At celebrations they danced to music played on a long wooden flute.

 The French Revolution

Soon after the settlers in North America had gained their independence, the people of France rose up against their king, Louis the Sixteenth. Under his rule, the poor had become even poorer and many people didn't have enough food to eat.

In 1789, in Paris, a crowd attacked a prison called the Bastille and the revolution began. The king was executed and the new government passed laws to give equal rights to everyone.

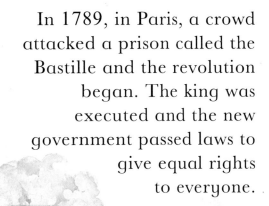

Amazing facts

Leonardo da Vinci was a great all-round genius of the Renaissance. He was a painter, sculptor, architect, engineer, scientist and mathematician.

Christopher Columbus sailed to America in 1492. But he believed he had travelled to the East Indies and was somewhere near Japan.

Louis the Fourteenth, King of France, ruled his country for longer than any other king or queen in Europe. He came to the throne when he was only five years old and ruled for 72 years.

The city of New York stands on the island of Manhattan. In 1626, a group of Dutch settlers bought the small island from a tribe of Native Americans for a chest of beads, some cloth and other trinkets.

The

industrial age

Coal and steam

About 200 years ago, machines powered by steam changed the way people lived and worked. Instead of farming and working in their homes, people moved into the towns to work in factories. This was the start of the Industrial Revolution.

The new machines burned lots of coal. Thousands of workers, including children, spent long days down the mines digging out the coal. At the surface, women sorted the coal into baskets and sacks. Mining was hard, dirty and often dangerous work.

The pioneers

The pioneers were men and women who left their homes on the east coast of North America to settle in the Far West. Groups of as many as 100 families set out together in wooden wagons hauled by oxen or horses.

Before finding their new
homes, the pioneers had
to face many dangers.
Many of them died of
hunger, drought and

freezing cold. Others were attacked by
Native Americans, who didn't want strangers
to settle on their hunting grounds.

Steam trains

Locomotives powered by steam pulled the first trains. Tunnels and bridges were built to take the new trains through hills and over rivers. Now people and goods could be moved about faster and more cheaply.

In 1869, the first railway to cross the United States of America from east coast to west coast was finished. The new railway brought thousands more people out to the West and helped settle this huge land.

Cars and planes

After the steam engine came the internal combustion engine. The internal combustion engine ran on petrol or diesel. This was the engine that drove cars and trucks, and powered the first aeroplanes.

The first cars didn't look much like modern cars and were very hard to drive. But by 1900, cars looked more like they do today. New air-filled tyres made them more comfortable and some cars could reach speeds of up to 130 kilometres an hour.

About the same time, the first aeroplanes took to the air. The Wright brothers flew the first aeroplane in 1903. In 1927, Charles Lindbergh was the first person to fly alone across the Atlantic Ocean.

World War I

In 1914, a great war broke out that lasted for four years. Many different countries were dragged into the war, which was called World War I.

During the war, soldiers fought from trenches that they had dug in the ground. By the end of the war, millions of soldiers had been killed.

Women played a very important part in the war. Many worked on farms and in factories while the men were away fighting. In the years after the war, women fought for and won the right to vote and to carry on working.

Life in the trenches was very hard. When it rained, the trenches became damp and muddy. Many soldiers got diseases such as trench foot from always wearing wet boots and socks.

In the home

New inventions began to make everyday life much easier. Some houses had hot and cold running water, and electric lighting became more common. People listened to the first radios, and telephones allowed them to talk to each other across long distances.

In many countries, children could now go to school to learn to read, write and count. New discoveries in medicine meant that doctors were able to cure diseases that had once killed thousands of people.

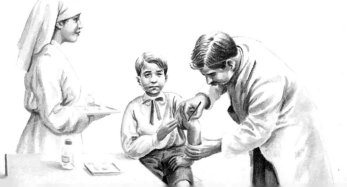

Revolution in Russia

In Russia, many people were unhappy
with the way the tsar ruled the country.
In 1917, a great crowd of workers and
soldiers marched to protest against
food shortages.

In the revolution that followed, the tsar abdicated and the Communist Party came to power under their leader, Lenin. The Communists wanted to set up a fairer system of government. In the name of the Russian people, they took control of most of the land, property and factories in the country.

■ World War II

In 1939, a second great war broke out that spread to almost every part of the world. This was World War II.

World War II was fought in Europe, in North Africa and in South-East Asia. In Europe, aeroplanes were used to bomb many cities, destroying millions of buildings and killing hundreds of thousands of people.

The war finally ended in 1945, when the first nuclear bombs were dropped on the Japanese towns of Hiroshima and Nagasaki.

▶ Powerful searchlights were used to pick out enemy aeroplanes as they flew over a city. Sirens blared and people ran for cover in air raid shelters.

Amazing facts

About 140 years ago, a tailor in San Francisco started making hard-wearing trousers for gold miners in California. His name was Levi Strauss and his trousers became known as jeans.

For many poor people living in Europe, the United States of America offered the possibility of a new and better life. Between 1830 and 1910, about 28 million Europeans sailed to the United States.

Thomas Edison was a famous American inventor who invented the phonograph: a machine that could play back recorded human voices. But his most important invention of all was probably the electric light bulb.

Today

The United Nations

After World War II, an organization was set up to help keep peace in the world. It was called the United Nations, or UN. Since then, the UN has been a place where all the countries of the world can meet and talk to one another. The UN also gives advice and money to help poorer countries improve their people's health and education.

Exploring Space

For thousands of years people had wondered what lay out in Space. In 1957, the first space probe, *Sputnik 1*, was launched into Space and circled around the Earth. Then in 1969, two astronauts landed on the Moon for the first time.

Astronauts can now
live and work in space
stations for
weeks at a time.
Scientists have
already sent
space probes to
land on Mars
and Venus.

Satellites out in
Space send
telephone and
television signals all
around the world.

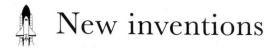 # New inventions

Ever since the first people discovered how to
make stone tools, human beings have been
inventing things that have changed the way
they live.

Today, we can fly
around the world in
just one and a half days, while computers
and machines do much of our work for us.
And people are still inventing new things.
What will we come up with next?

Amazing facts

Since 1945, many new nations have been formed. There are now over 190 nations in the world.

The Hubble Space Telescope is the biggest telescope in Space. This powerful telescope can send us pictures of stars and galaxies that cannot be seen by telescopes on the Earth.

In the last 100 years, there have been more developments in science and technology than in the previous 4,000 years.

INDEX

Aborigine 90
aeroplane 102, 103, 110
Africa 20, 38, 50, 68-69,
    78, 88, 89, 110
Akbar 73
Allah 51
America 70, 78, 84, 86,
    87, 88, 89, 94, 98,
    101, 112
animal 15, 16, 17, 18,
    20, 90
Arabia 50
archaeologist 7, 8
armour 62, 66
art 20, 49, 68, 73, 76, 90
astronaut 116, 117
astronomy 51, 76
Athens 35
Australia 90-91
Aztecs 70-71, 74

Babylon 22
barbarians 46-47
barley 25

beer 25
Beijing 64, 65
Benin 68
Boston Tea Party 86
bread 25
bridge 100
Buddhism 31

California 112
canal 71
car 102
caravel 78, 79
carrack 79
castle 54-55, 62
catamaran 32
cathedral 49, 58
cave 14, 20
ceremony 19, 67, 68, 71
China 64-65, 74
Christian Church 58-59
Christianity 42-43
city 22, 35, 40, 48, 49,
    51, 64, 71, 110
clay 19, 22
cloth 25, 65

clothes 14, 17, 19, 112
coal 96
coin 44
Colosseum 44
Columbus, Christopher
Communists 109
computer 119
Constantinople 48, 49
cotton 88
craftsman 49, 53, 58, 65

East Indies 94
Edison, Thomas 112
Egypt 24-25, 26-27, 28
Egyptian Empire 24
Egyptians 24-25, 26-27, 44
electric light 107, 112
Elizabeth the First 80
empire 24, 38, 39, 42,
    43, 46, 47, 48, 64, 70,
    72, 73
engine 102
England 80, 84, 85, 86, 87
Europe 38, 46, 52, 54,
    58, 76, 78, 79, 80, 81,
    85, 110, 112
explorers 78-79, 90

Factory 96, 104, 109
farmers 25, 52
farming 18, 54, 85, 96, 104
Far West 98, 101
fire 15, 16, 19
flax 25
food 15, 16, 18, 25, 62
Forbidden City 65
Forum 40
France 93, 94
French Revolution 92-93

Gladiator 44
god 26, 29, 30, 36, 37,
    42, 51, 71, 73
Great Wall of China 74
Greece 34-35, 36-37

Hebrews 28-29
Hinduism 30, 73
Hiroshima 110
historian 7, 19, 20, 44
history 7
house 14, 16, 62, 83, 107
Hubble Space
    Telescope 120
hunting 16, 17

Incas 70
India 30-31, 72, 78
Industrial Revolution 96
invention 107, 112
irrigation 25
Islam 50
Israel, Kingdom of 28

Japan 66-67, 74, 94, 110
Jesus 42, 43
joust 56

King 58, 68, 78, 80, 81,
   82, 85, 86, 93, 94,
knight 56-57, 62
Kremlin 82, 83

Lenin 109
Leonardo da Vinci 94
Lindbergh, Charles 103
locomotive 100
longship 52
lord 54, 56
Louis the Fourteenth 81, 94
Louis the Sixteenth 93

Machine 96, 119
Manhattan 94
medicine 51, 107
merchant 22, 48
Mesopotamia 22, 28
Mexico 70
Middle Ages 54, 58, 62
Middle East 22, 46
Moguls 72-73, 74
monk 58
Moscow 82, 83
mosque 51
Muhammad 50
mummy 27
Muslim 50-51, 73

Nagasaki 110
nao 79
Native American 84, 85,
   94, 99
navigation 32, 78
New York 94
nuclear bomb 110
nun 58

Oba 68
Olympic Games 36

Pacific Ocean 32, 90
palace 49, 64, 65, 72, 81, 82
Palestine 42
paper 25
papyrus 25
Parthenon 35
peasant 54
people, early 16-17, 20
people, the first 14-15, 20, 118
Peru 70
pharaoh 26-27, 44
Philip the Second 81
phonograph 112
pioneers 98-99
Polynesians 32-33
porcelain 65
printing 77
pyramid 26

Queen 78, 80, 81, 94

Radio 107
railway 101
religion 19, 20, 27, 29, 30, 31, 36, 37, 42, 43,

50, 51, 58, 71, 73
Renaissance 76-77, 78, 94
revolution 93, 108, 109
road 39
Roman Empire 38-39, 40, 41, 42, 43, 46, 47, 48
Romans 38-39, 40-41, 42
Rome 38, 39, 40, 44
Russia 82-83, 108-109
Russian Revolution 108-109

Sailor 32, 34, 78
samurai 66, 74
satellite 117
school 41, 58, 107
science 76, 120
scientist 44, 51, 90, 117
settler 84-85, 86, 87, 88, 94
shelter 14, 16
ship 52, 53, 78, 79, 85
shop 61
Siddhartha Gautama 31
silk 65

slave 41, 88, 89
slavery 88-89
soldier 38, 54, 55, 56, 104, 105
South-East Asia 110
Space 116-117, 120
space probe 116, 117
space station 117
Spain 50
steam 96, 100
steam train 100
Stonehenge 19
sugar 85, 88

Taj Mahal 74
tea ceremony 67
technology 120
telephone 107, 117
telescope 120
television 117
temple 30, 35, 40, 71
Tenochtitlán 70, 71
theatre 37
tobacco 85, 88
tools 15, 17, 19, 20, 118
town 60-61, 96
trade 22, 34, 44, 48, 85
truck 102

tsar 82, 108, 109
tunnel 100
Tutankhamun 27, 44

United Nations 114
United States of America 87, 101, 112

Vikings 52-53
village 19, 54
vote 104

Wagon 98
war 54, 55, 56, 66, 104, 110, 114
War of Independence 86-87
warrior 50, 52, 66
weapon 7, 17
West Indies 78
wheat 25, 34
wool 18, 19
World War I 104-105
World War II 110-111, 114
Wright brothers 103
writing 22

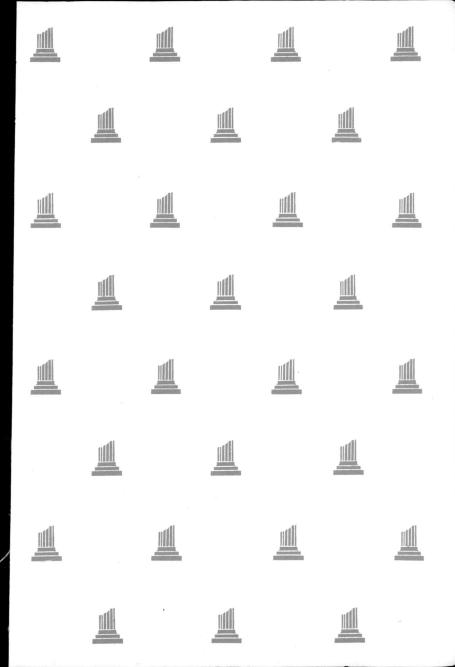